The Things
We Don't Know

Also by Toni Thomas:

Chosen
        Brick Road Poetry Press

Fast as Lightening
        Gribble Press

Walking on Water
        Finishing Line Press

Blue Halo
        Annalese Press

Ace Raider of the Unfathomable Universe
        Annalese Press

You'll be Fast as Lightning Coveting my Painted Tail
        Annalese Press

Hotsy Totsy Ballroom
        Annalese Press

Love Adrift in the City of Stars
        Annalese Press

In the Pink Arms of the City
        Annalese Press

In the Kingdom of Longing
        Annalese Press

The Things We Don't Know

Poems

First published in 2021 by Annalese Press
134 Towngate
Netherthong
Holmfirth
West Yorkshire HD9 3XZ
England

Copyright © 2021 Toni Thomas

Please Note
All characters and situations appearing
in these pages are in the service of poetry.
Any resemblance to real persons,
living or dead, is purely coincidental.

All rights reserved. No part of this publication may be reproduced, stored, or transmitted in any form, or by any means electronic, mechanical or photo-copying, recording or otherwise, without the express written permission of the publisher.

Cover by Peter Wadsworth
Cover image: The Orange Gatherers by
J.W. Waterhouse

British Library Cataloguing-in-Publication Data
A catalogue record for this book is available on request from the British Library.

ISBN 978-1-9163620-4-8

Contents

Part One: *Preeminence*

The scrim of the dark	3
She cups her words	4
The girl in the blue coat	5
It was cumbersome	6
The girl nibbling pistachios	7
We fled and fled	8
The Calgary Sisters Club	9
Over time you start to deny	11
You conspire to save me	12
Winter wears its weight	13
What I knew was a small thing	14
When the first words came	16
Perhaps at some point	17
We pocketed the dust	18
The bishop of strict things	19
Now that the blight has set in	20
The pussy willows I passed as a child	21

Part Two: *Appetite*

The man covers the bare head of the sun	25
You have a check list	26
We are dishing out cards	27
Did you always believe	28
Out of the forest spilled a sickly green	29
You have a habit of acting smart	30
Appetite	31
Not everyone at Alison's party	33

When you came with your polished orchestra	34
You brought your wants	35
The dark has grown pebbled seams	36
You track brilliance	37
I am perched on the bed	38
Talking about *the Problem*	39
You are wearing your dilapidated riding jacket	40
I know the world isn't always made of brokenness	41
Had we subscribed to the pay as you go	42

PART THREE: *Snow*

Does the day's wet saga	47
When you supposition hope	48
You had a sermon	49
Did Orpheus come	50
If the girl wages war on your bible	51
Are there destinies we forget	52
You cull harsh verbs	53
The light is slant	54
How do I make a testament to my losses	55
Early morning, Newport	56
In the backyard version of my life	57
And what if the palest fathom	58
When I scrape death	60
The dark stirs amid the sedge	61
Last night I housed a newsroom	62
I am picking off lice	63
The onion field half wants	64
Some days the shade leaves me	65
I have summoned the dark	66

PART FOUR: *Flame*

You still believe in fairies	71
We were being coerced	72
We propagate stories	73
She is wearing her palomino shoes	74
The holly that has scratched its mark	75
We opened the gates	76
In the penitentiary of desire	77
Troubles drop on my pillow	78
We have come single file	79
She had resurrected a pole star	80
The rain won't let up	81
In the mythology of my life	83
After a while	84
How to Make Love	85
My mother captured everything	87
My arm is the arm dead folks write on	89
We are gathering honeysuckle	90
The earth is turning light	91
Have you seen the eye of God waving	92

*What shall I do singer and first-born
in a world where the deepest black is grey
and inspiration is kept in a thermos?
With all this immensity
in a measured world?*

Marina Tsvetaeva

Part One

Preeminence

The scrim of the dark

holds a green girl in a dyed uniform.
She wants to save things
call lament out of its cramped corset.

Nobody has told her the dark
traffics in greed
not every voice is a home.

In the clear hours
she fries egg, tomato
tailgates her fantasy lover
the one in loose pants
who sculpts women
recites Holderlin, Rilke
the tiger lilies petaled prayers.

The girl wants to travel things
beyond a clipped room
synthetic housedress

find the man alive
showered clean
in an open bathrobe.

She cups her words

sprinkles them over the parched garden
cinquefoil   recumbent   jocular   polestar
spreads them like lumps of manure
hopes they take hold
spell out a different scenery.

Her father has always confirmed
the sideways in her, the too many flaws
an angular life that only barely
comes decent.

She has learned to walk slow, listen
spill words
soft as a broken sacrament
see where they land

which mascara the dark
hostage a fork
scratch the walls naked

which map a meal ticket
scarab the house
get ransacked
rain pummeled
smooched

which ones
in decent weather
grow a pear tree.

The girl in the blue coat

has made a bargain with death
but is not saying
goes around with a tumbler
crooked words
a pandemic's meal ticket

stews in the dark
invents stories
catalogs the lovers who got away
children invaded by poachers.

It is June when weeds declare
their preeminence
spread wide as pancakes
overtake the common ground of her yard.

So tell me, in the story
she invents about vice grips
a stolen house
does the girl stitch her hands blind
carry a sack on her back
pots and pans, a thimble

will the wolf wax cunning
eat her up in a fit of rage
or will her body be pressed
by the wind's kisses
turn out to be
the pale seed
pried open
about to be born?

It was cumbersome

hoisting my suitcases through the Land of Oz
following a brick road no longer yellow.

My shoes were brown, thick
hit the ground, wanted to splash.
I'd packed two summer dresses, a rayon wrap
just in case you decided to marry me.

It was cumbersome carrying my this and thats
canister of blue pens
crippled fantasy of a bright sunset.

You claim sometimes I steal loneliness
from the dark's crib set
my words can't be trusted
stay decent weight in a land of foam.

The clothes stuffed in my suitcase
a sermon of wrinkles
too many books, a hairbrush
avenue of thread.

What could I do but hope for the best
imagine you willing
the bright troubadour under a damp moon
in the garden of loss
the one who sings.

The girl nibbling pistachios

doesn't know the dark can speak whiplash
purge her faith inside the bodies of men
who come and go as false prophets

waitresses at The Green Onion
waits on a man to love
shared garden of cosmos, splash pool
waits on June when the tourists arrive
leave good tips
order steak and oysters
instead of the Blue Plate Special.

The girl has hair the color of chestnuts
hands somebody must want
stubby fingers that can scope pain
file it away in a suitcase
know how to keep promises
others forget.

The girl won't suck your breath dry
make the sun into a pallbearer
crumble your words
then eat them
has learned how to wait
serve up the best plate of hash browns
eggs, streaky bacon
spoon feed your lips
around more than the
sum of a breakfast.

We fled and fled

sayonara sludge seated past
with your ass brazen
sayonara girl in a hiccup
plastic bubble
sayonara coat of arms
in a spineless play
sayonara child in the field
aimless amid the butterflies.

We fled and fled
drank up the sunset
loaded our pockets with soporific candy
licked men, money, houses, cars
podcasts, barbells, spike heels, eyeliner
the bronzed tan, model's skinny

we fled and fled
from crop shares to city
gobbled words, relationships, geography
gobbled hellos, goodbyes
gobbled the dark till it spoke silky
turned the future into a king sized bed.

The Calgary Sisters Club

was something started three years ago
when we grew bored with rolling down hills
when our parents were in their elsewheres
when June sat heat stunned with its
park sprinkler, melted toys.

Decked in cowgirl hats, red bandanas
we practiced being champion riders
stunt girls nobody could beat
the ones who ride bareback
stand up and wave
slip so low you can feel the dust
fly under our boots.
Every bull rider on the rodeo circuit
wanted to marry us
make us their hullabaloo, prize possession
but my mother had already cautioned me
to hold out in the name of art
for something different.

The Calgary Sisters Club was made
for girls like me
whose lives are less than perfect
the ones with broken homes
cramped apartments
no car to get to the big store
spy the ocean
buy a strapless dress.

What could I do but practice agility
learn to lasso an aberrant animal
turn swagger into something more than
the prize stud on horseback

become the girl who tames things
melts men, pistols
takes the world's defeats
turns them into a bright palomino?

Over time you start to deny

the big slice of cake
settle for the small one
want me to do the same
in the name of a slim waist

roam my split ends
mess of tangle
sermon about men
the need to take hold
make myself tasty
not just the girl in a paper dress
squeezing words out of rust.

I have been trained to practice
good penmanship, turn the other cheek
marry Jesus
not let the peril of cake deter
turn my father's rage into petals.

You settle for the thin slice of cake
no ice cream
defend the eye of the scale
school me in the popularized landscape
how to pick lice off pale skin
be the perky Priscilla in a yellow dress.

But I am sixteen.
Unknown to this household will grow up
take no man by the thick of his throat
feed him precious bread, honey
let him bulldoze the dark
thick as a tyrant.

You conspire to save me

tutor on the hazard of houses
crew cut lawns
streets with too many cars, stifled voices
clip magazine pics of Paris, Berlin, London
tack them to the wall.

Over time I grow leery
of the destinies you impose
afraid I'll fall from grace
drop out of school
settle for a cramped flat, desk job
four children and a hungry man.

Sometimes my body doesn't fit
I eat angel food cake, then diet
the name of god dangles on a shoestring
I want to kiss you
don't know how.

Stuffed inside
somebody else's spike heels
it can be hard to know what to do
who to turn to
when early a.m., still young
you fall across the parquet floor
shatter the weight
of your morning tea cup
drown.

Winter wears its weight

prickly, thin skinned
wears its weight
in hand me downs
maybes
that spring will paste back
the fallen fairy tale
spit the girl out
let moonstruck lovers dance
unsinged across flame.

When the midwife says *you're pregnant*
what can I do
a pauper's suitcase
plastic wrapped windows
his disdain?

Winter wears its weight
heavy as a country in mourning.
And I know this place
its thick coat, mute keys
the provisional of April
mud smacked roads.

I buy three planters
dig in begonia, geranium, lobelia
call them *our garden*
as if loss is more than a
squat landscape
even fledging buds
can rise up
turn out to be
the first delight of my newborn.

What I knew was a small thing

propped memory
slip of paper in a secret glove
tremble of bell
flower inked on the palm
tiny castle dug in a sand tray

what I knew wasn't a matter
of the world's steeples
luck or money or scrutiny
wasn't fated to be the marauder
hiding behind a blue veil

what I knew was wordless
the quiet sunrise
language of trees
hummingbird's pause at the feeder
grown back poppies
first dazzle of snow
nameless ballerina alive on the jewel box
swirl of the bathwater
sheep at the fence
slow sung lullaby
wet kiss.

If I was oblivious
to the defeats
the mistreated migrants
maimed animals
the way people can live amid death
not claim it

too young to crowd the dark
stuff it in my suitcase
press allegiance to any one flag

perhaps it was something deeper
truer back then that carried me
insisted we lick grass
swim with guppies
wrap the sunset around our shoulders
warm as a coat

let me lull in the pool of your eyes
spy the feast table
the autumn leaves decked in red gloves
the old couple practicing their polka
before all the afterwards set in
the crowbars and conceit
crowd pleasing.

When the first words came

they must have been joyous
mama   dog   cake   papa   play
must have been short, unarmed
able to capture the curve of the bridge
rubber pool, cookie, stuffed toy

when the first words came
they must have felt fragile
festooned in a wobbly boat
ribboned with eyelet
eager to spin and lurch
in the sea's meadow

when the first words came
they must have flirted a new planet
ruby red, luminous
Saturn's dazzle of rings

felt like the trees waving
the baby bouncer lifting us
higher and higher
to where the stars sip sugar milk
every song is a gold canary.

Perhaps at some point

I'd been trained to beg favors
bargain
my mock ruby ring for your rubber frog
caramel custard in exchange for the brownie
a red wagon instead of the blue one

perhaps at some point everything seemed possible
the corner store loaded with ice cream
inflatable pool that never turns flat.

We devoured pop tarts, lemon ices
billboards with platters of pie
frosted pink cocktails
swore we'd be pertinent, timely
the ones with fleet shoes
no mess-ups.

Perhaps at some point
we were trained to beg favors
display our good grades, diploma
slip into designer clothes, the pert voice
angle our life bright as a stage set.

Each time you sat at the table
I read you the Bill of Rights
offered up my fabricated sunset
girl in a zippered coat.

Perhaps at one point
you thought you would marry me
till the sky started falling
and the wind, the waves
so many waves.

We pocketed the dust

from the moon
till our skirts were loaded
with powder and phosphorous.
It was hard to move forward
but we tried

ate the sodden peas
bolted cabbage
memorized words
in case they got lost
and fantasy lovers, family
the names of the dead

memorized species of trees
the vanity of men
maiden fern and lady slippers
bramble
the way blackberry bushes
bloody your skin
before they reward
with the slush of pulp.

It was the time of upheaval
when no future is certain.
You dug through my pockets
in search of candy
I spelt my mother's name
with a chalk stick.
Every lost room
was a homage to poems.

The bishop of strict things

stares down the morning's sermon
of forsythia, bilberries
carves god into the face of the tree
corrals the river into a font.

The girl swings from a sodden rope
over the embankment
forgets she's a weak swimmer
summer of attrition.

Will the rope hold
will the river welcome her as
more than a thrash of limbs
broken chalice
float her down the length of its body
past the destitute houses
blue epistles
make treasure
out of the world's rust?

Now that the blight has set in

is anyone warring
complaining about the lack of meat
burnt toast, blind future
the way the sun tilts
the rain turns thrifty

is anyone fighting about the swing set
radio news, vacation
who gets to phantom the dark
unbury the blue soldier?

My little boy plays doctor
bandages wounded animals
fills our dog's ear with a drum beat
shuffles cards
remembers the summer's prize melon
my botched orange hair
the kitten carried away by possum.

Afternoons we bake cake
dust with powdered sugar
cut the cake into slices
offer them to the night's cramped fist
to the neighbor child who stays alone
stares out the window
whose life has never been able
to grow a pear tree.

The pussy willows I passed as a child

never asked for anything
scoured my pocket
for the right word
bribe of coin

needed to be owned
cut, worshiped
preserved

were a velvet clutch
pale continence
of an ancient poem.

Sometimes I'd ambition
a keepsake
beyond my father's voice

snap a branch or two
steal them away
in my backpack

stall them forever
in a glass vase
pronounced deathless.

Part Two

Appetite

The man covers the bare head of the sun

with his armpit
wants no fortune teller's universe
blazing rival.

Afterwards things turn inky
shriveled crops
an empty house
city in ruin.

The man devises plans
pitches his brand name
offers up a new planet
for after this one.

Is it possible when the man
fabricates luck
twists his will into a spaceship
not everyone will call him a hero

the sun will snap free
threaten to scorch
send out its army of giants?

You have a check sheet

like to tally
count up success
pinch words till they bleed

claim my score is a pittance
speaks of lazy bones
a slump urchin
sea of commas.

After this I try to look different
straight pin my posture
recite Nietzsche, Goethe
postmodernism
a treatise on the sex life of cows.

See how I flirt with the rain
don't get wet
splash flowers onto a renegade page
attempt to be the tasty pecan
in your back pocket
the one never beheaded by fog
forced to eat gruel with the giants.

We are dishing out cards

you strategize
aim for the aces
flash a winning hand
chalk up the points.

I have seen you sidestep disease
impending disaster
make mush into a dinner of grilled fish
have seen you shuffle the cards
slide them out of your shirt sleeve
till your hand spills kings
conquest.

If love was a matter of sleight of hand
the mastery of cards
you'd think I'd have learned
a thing or two by now
how to knit the hearts to the spades
sing with a pearled voice
host a family of trumps
keep my plumage vested

you'd think I'd know how to turn myself
from lowly dwarf
into queen.

Did you always believe

nice girls inherit the earth
want to please
leak only sun into your trousers
bake succulent casseroles
plum cake
call down no troubled moon
in a casket

did you always believe
they never sully their voice
speak in the rhetoric of rattles
never haul dead weight
the leftovers of a breakfast?

Is it true when you married me
you needed to be the polestar
worshipped for your immaculate
an intelligence beyond saviors

that under your strict eye
my voice turned ragged
every flower was forced to dine
in a blue hearse?

Out of the forest spilled a sickly green

the green of embittered peas
moldy bread, cheese gone rancid
the green of girls without a home, coat
the green of sledged words, stymied ones
excrement and mud.

Out of the forest spilled a caustic green
the kind that glazes the body of dying animals
the kind no one wants to make a trouser set
live in.

I ran back to the house
told my father about the blood
the hillside's stoned refractory
the topple of ancient limbs
stripped bark
cemetery of briars

but out of the corner of his eye
I saw no verdant meadow
the last of the maiden fern
had already fled.

You have a habit of acting smart

the knowing landscape
arrive with a fistful of morning
refuse to go empty
pedestrian my wants
till I am the trite girl
in a dust dress.

In this world
things never look manhandled
even when the head of my porcelain doll
gets crushed
left for rot in the sick room
you show off your shiny
claim she had age working against her
you'll find a replacement.

We try to appear decent.
I am leery, lovesick
go along with the enterprise
oil my limbs like a rusty toy.
After all, we have two children, a home
nobody wants to see things shatter
do they?

When you accidentally
crack the head of my doll
place her in the sick room
return to your late night emails
I am stunned at how undeterred
you move past my tears
nest all those other women
inside the neat valley
of your fictions.

Appetite

The impostor sex idol
you inhabit a sizzle hotel
marry your lips to mary janes
red hots and tootsies
periwinkles splashed in a sea of dots
bliss babies and sixlets
slide kiwi bisque ice cream
into a waffle cone
avalanche with gummies

bundle the crumbs
stash me in your pocket
devour late night in the trash heap
when the moon blisters
the dark turns a specious bride.

Later you come back for more
paw thighs
the slope of legs
more chew
more caramel
Belgian chocolate
daredevils
sweet and sour
move in and out of the wrappers
as if we are tinted cocktails
nylon stockings wiggled into a lunchbox.

And as for *me* –
what can I say about my willing
the way I curse and resist
tease then wet nurse

wear my crotch ample as snowdrops
watch you pickpocket
squeeze each and every macaroon cluster
snug to your lips
devour.

Not everyone at Alison's party

took her seriously
the benign and the daggers
the aerial landscape
twinkle lights on a blue terrace.

Not everyone called her name agreeable
propped her on a velvet cushion
soft soothed
offered their willing
instead of mace.

There was paucity
a pawned sunset
too many words oozing chocolate

her name spangled then gashed
till we hardly knew it.

When you came with your polished orchestra

recitation of names
the milk jug's flirty
over the confirmation of roses
recalled Dante, Chaucer
the Latin name for every plant, flower
showed me your neat rows of books
squash, butter beans, cilantro

practiced your vast knowledge of trees
what did I know of the politician's
uneven handshake
the way the dark leaks

what did I know of men
who search the bright nest egg
pleasure in crushing it
with their motherless feet?

You brought your wants

to my dinner table.
At first they squatted low in a blue disguise
modest plate
willingly ate my sautéed carrots, cabbage
willingly navigated the crumbs of the toast

but over time they took up more room
insisted on dill, lamb, crème brulee
the complex wine
good brandy.

You brought your wants
wrapped them in cellophane
feigned discreet, the generous guest
not the one who insists
keeps a score card
slashes.

Over time the lava beds set in
birds up on a hook with their necks snapped
the classy linen and call girls

till my supper table looked a pale thing
archaic even
its bread and tomato
as if God dines only with the rich
will not suffer a cheap bowl
of noodles.

The dark has grown pebbled seams

wears a devious tongue
might snatch the moon of its silver.

I sit up in bed
trace the stars with my finger
listen to crickets
the fallen breath of the sun
listen to adults argue then kiss
the night move in creased trousers

no need to go anywhere
be someone
my nightdress sheer against my skin
that tickle of breeze climbing the window.

I tell you the dark has grown pebbled seams
holds its breath
over what you are about to do to me
holds its breath.

You track brilliance

pamper youth in a glass jar
stabbed with honey.
I have seen others
gussy up to your sweet talk
rub their thighs along
your body's pearled hem

but winter abolishes petals
turns the road slick as an ice rink.
You were lecturing about beauty
childishness
botox and acclaim
the need to take hold
amount to something

who would have thought
come January
I'd spin off that curve
slide head on into the coming car
end up a factory of stitches

who would have thought
you'd disappear
through the revolving door
never look back.

I am perched on the bed

travel my attempt at a romance language
with the French dictionary
a middle aged tutor.

Words slide in and out
knock head, rub thighs, roam the river
musee gets mixed up with *moules*
bon jour with *au revoir*.

I have spent a lifetime coaxing words
out of a hidden mattress
calming their limbs
to keep the dark from ripping.

Monsieur says I am *d'un eleve mediocre*
the working class girl who flirts but never comes
that no tutor will ever manage to train me
the art of nuance is beyond my skein.

I am trying to mouth things
as more than a hacked word
polished suitcase
Parisian tart
coax you to show me
your frailest petal, unhinged voice
as if nothing is beyond reclaim
goodness rests
on a sea of snow.

But you do not listen
thread the knot of your noose
bit by bit
decide I am dull
the hapless girl in a crushed pastiche
that no dictionary, French tutor
can ever make up for a bad education.

Talking about *the Problem*

when life hits you in the face
and you don't want to be sad
the hours of your sleep clipped away
the house a penance of shambles
no dog food, bread, milk, eggs

when you talk a mile a minute
chatterbox
try to keep things buoyant
even if nobody is listening
run out with no bra, panties
proclaim your sexy in a gift box

everything in wait
the days of content
a gamble of mischief

till finally the other shoe kicks in
the dented one with the crushed toes
pitted heel
too despondent to say anything

the one that stops limp
in the middle of the street
lays out like a crucifix
ready to be mown over
by any ordinary truck.

You are wearing your dilapidated riding jacket

the one I thought you'd left behind
thick shouldered with leather buttons
a shaped waist
cuffs too threadbare to claim you

are digging up roots
determined to transplant the poppies
save the rosemary
from the lawnmower's blade.

I have seen you go out
drink down the rain
spread eagle
sopping wet by the yard shed
have seen you crush grass
under your bare feet
watch it spring back
loyal as a lover.

You are wearing your dilapidated jacket
the corduroy one
that has seen better days
was once the deep green
of the forest

back then, when your life was
ribboned hair fanning the meadow
when the world knew you
the horses hadn't fled.

I know the world isn't always made of brokenness

anger so hostile it maims the ship
casts greed over the territory of a house.

I know there are marriage albums
that last a lifetime
don't shuffle in soaked shoes
that the coat of the dark boasts ancient thread
my smallest wish can get crushed or
just as easily rise up on an April day.

I know how to call down hope from a leaky ledge
feed it cake, the small word, night dress
know there is more than the man
who straps down his wife
rams his forehead into her face over and over
breaks her nose, calls her *deserving*

know there is more than this bleeding.

Had we subscribed to the pay as you go

version of love
the one that sidles up to your door
boasts sizzle and midnight
never condemns with a fist?

It can be pitiful watching me squirm
offer up my ecclesiastics
over a crushed future
while off in the distance
the city burns in a blue haze.

The year my lustrous
chestnut hair got shaved
no one was willing to talk famine
summer starved of its barbeque
strapless dresses

so we convinced ourselves
things stall but grow back
the maimed field is never just
a destitution of wings
marriage invaded by cancer.

Part Three

Snow

Does the day's wet saga

pierce your heart
taunt over torn things
the drowned field, lost migrants
orphaned words gone muck rack

does it make you lament
the mute woman stalled at her window
the spine of the roof ripped bare of shingle

does the day's wet saga
ruin your plans for the picnic
swamp the grass
pool the graves in the cemetery
make for a valley of rain
ocean of castoffs

does it damp down hope
the provisional lampshade
turn the girl's oyster shells of longing
into a palm of rust?

When you supposition hope

offer it up your crab cakes
shrimp cocktail
Bavarian strudel
promise to behave
comb your words careful
not traitor the sun
for being a turncoat

when you supposition hope
tease it into a slinky dress
dazzle in the dark earrings

be prepared for the hazardous
the ripped open house
ransacked children

prepared to rethink
the color of emptiness
why the girl in the fantasy landscape
felt forced to turn blind.

You had a sermon

it kept repeating in my ear
repeat repeat repeat
till I gained the agility
of a parrot
could voice box back
anything you dished out

repeat repeat repeat.

You had a sermon
it was crimson and nosegays
boxed ears
a soiled prayer book.

Over time I could wind the world
snug around my finger
not let it fray

coax ash into a blazing bush
shape your guttural sounds
into a chorus.

Did Orpheus come

slow, ungainly
the white cup of his shirt
echoing the lily
offer to sponge death
empire the daisies
place chords in my ear
more sonorous than a sunset

did you come here
divested of things
not to cross the marbled bridge
but to sing from it
your voice a bag of nothing
pearled with the day?

If the girl wages war on your bible

creases its seams
peels the grass of your tomb
will the sermon on the mount tilt
the parched pages give up their braille

will you strip away her only coat
job at the diner
make her beg for mercy
loiter counterfeit at dusk
by the Merrimack River

if the girl no longer wages war
finds a way to calm things
will the whippoorwills call
the day halt its house of tears

will you come to her
no admission ticket
contract for this or that
till she stops minding the burrs
puts them to sleep in a silver ocean
all the pages of her life
open at last?

Are there destinies we forget

that are more than puffed pantomimes
the girl in a gilded dress
who must stand up on tiptoe
force words into caviar

are there destinies that get lost
the misplaced dream, absent lover
foreign country
landslide that buries our suitcase

signs that beg to be noticed
no, not this man but that one
no, not this house, this job, this life
but we are busy
minding the pert details of the world

are there destinies we forget
that long to live in us
tempt and tickle under the bed sheets
offer to turn the wanton sky
into clover

scratch in the dark
fierce
till we listen?

You cull harsh verbs

callow ones
spiny treatises, bramble
strip the metal future

cull pale wishes
blue algae, the iced lullaby
boy stirring dust in his palm

cull hurried daybreak
the flattened path to the well
sinners and prophets
the forgotten, the seized

cull declarative sentences
olives stabbed red with pimento
the clear-cut forest
orphaned vows

ride hotshot over every swollen line
blue swagger
mow down the past
till it is fragile
invite the grass to return
thick as a deathbed.

The light is slant

if the sea has wounds
colossal as its silvered skin
are they only the carnage
of a chastened eye missing?

Gulls screech and dive
watch the wind crease waves
a boy skim on his wakeboard
the old woman walk the sand
warbly as a truck.

The light is slant.
It is easier now to give things up
cast them off as last year's swimsuit
stop inking words on my palm
like *surplus, fidelity, provisional, success*
easier to turn the tide
eat at the servant's table
prosper the simple bowl of oatmeal.

The light is slant
gulls watch things come and go
families, apartments, jobs, cars, lovers
watch as the soldier on the mount weeps
the eye of the sun fans the rain
then scorches.

How do I make a testament to my losses

thread them into the hem of my coat
rename their sob stories
crushed orchids, defeat
speak to them as if the night
holds a handrail
never just squanders

how do I decipher the tree's parables
set your clothes above the racks of ruin
spell your name in my palm
as more than a wrecking crew
soiled house

hold you precious

as if even the losses we inherit
are mere gusts of wind
the field's desire to lick snow?

Early morning, Newport

the sky dissolves into the ocean
a grey-blue vastness shrouds the hills.

Daku once said *loneliness is an empty pot*
feathered by God's fingers
as if out of nothing
gulls arrive
the fog lifts.

Once I thought vastness laid
only in strongly defined surfaces
didn't notice how the sky
gives itself over
the sea receives.

In the backyard version of my life

waits a small girl with a suitcase.
She speaks tenuous
doesn't yet know the ancient name
for sump grass, swallow, cottonwood
doesn't yet know
the death camp of trees.

In the backyard version
blue willow plates escape for a picnic
lovers waltz under the moon
bugs of the dark
buzz with fluorescent fruit

my patched coat emblems the sunset
I know how to forgive critics
drink from the milk maid's cup
rescue a crushed vowel.

In the backyard version of my life
that is less beggarly
you wait
with your hay field
succulent seasons
hoarfrost and heat

every raised bed
calls my name
till I am more than clumps of weed
fingerlings and plastic roses
the woodcutter's shaved body.

And what if the palest fathom

of the heart's namesake
opened itself up
smoothed down the spiny places
overgrown trellis, makeshift rooms
spoke to me in a whisper
shared confidence

and what if the world opened up
the cruise ship of the soul's cargo
my dinner of aubergines, onion on the stove
the coat on the sideboard in need of a mend
and what if it called my name
sat down
refused the offer of dead roses

could I allow myself
such infinite repose, not turn away
the clothes outside on the line drying
the day hung like pearled beads
across a violent landscape
nothing cursed beyond
the measure of my reclaim?

When the night sets in
there will still be drownings
tucked away lynch knots
the child adrift with no meal
serpent winds that shackle the shingle

but who in their right mind
fallen half a degree from beauty
could not resist this newfound confidence
arrived on such a quiet wing, stealthy
want to settle in, offer up lemon cake, ginger

remake the dark into a more joyous creature
who would not come more whole cloth
more willing to this table
then me?

When I scrape death

with my thumbnail
attempt to pry it loose
exfoliate

will it listen
set up a trust fund
make me the beneficiary
bend my tongue away from
his valley of fictions

will it travel my flimsy dress
make the caterpillars leap
the child give up her raincoat

when I call death out of hiding
threaten to scratch its eyes
will it turn rueful

leave me stranded
in a bland alley
on a bald faced day

or milk me of every idle concern
I have ever managed to muster

speak to me once and for all
beyond the language of loss?

The dark stirs amid the sedge

threatens to vandalize
my house of sand
searches for me
vagrant among the poppies.

Tell me – if the night
leaves me for dead
will you still come back
wounded but not exiled

hold up my heart
as if I am morning star
newly chalked petal

open my body
to the bee's thirst
the hummingbird's nectar

cup my face
help me carry your cross
through the fields
weightless?

Last night I housed a newsroom

in my ear
hard facts, famine
displaced people

slept with the ocean
her rhythmic and thunder
fluted shells
seaweed
crushed stone

last night I dreamt you
in my ear
watched your pale horse
ride across the muscle
of my sky's plain

the madrones sway
wet mouth of the waves
bury the sand
in reckless kisses

last night I slept with you.

I am picking off lice

stale crumbs, old words
the lobotomist's nameplate
picking off layers of wallpaper
flagrant promises, deluded ones

picking off cruel winds, the recalcitrant
lovers who marry their lips
to mind fields, industry
wear the death of conceit

picking off stale days, chipped ones
seasons scalded by sun
burdened with winter.

You call out to me
from the other world
encourage me to fuse my life
to a plush bathrobe
but what do you know about girls
with tar pitch on their tongue
nobody around to protect them

what do you remember about pistols
his hands turned dangerous
how he could rob a girl of her body
her voice
turn her into a valley of holes
grin?

The onion field half wants

to be noticed
but the cars don't care
nor the lives bent on speed
shiny nameplates
expensive leather.

Will the onion field stay patient
able to last
still offer up her slender blades
intricate balls of crystal
set up a dinner table
in the middle of dirt
for you, for me
let the eye of the dark claim
not curse those who pickpocket
turn the sun brittle?

Mornings when the fog comes
erases the onion field's face
when dust mounts
the rain threatens
will you still remember us
stay faithful?

Some days the shade leaves me

speechless
I pick dragonflies
out of a blue net.
Your hands are faded
as a crucifix.
Everything gets pronounced
wrong in me.

Some days nothing holds up.
The dark traffics in road kill
conceit.

But if the river runs dry
where will I travel to
how will I rise up beyond
this burning bush
speak?

I have summoned the dark

but it hardly speaks
is full of thorns, misnomers
carries a carcass, shaved moon

have summoned your words
their prickly skin, escape hatches
summoned love with its cankers
turned over stones of perdition
that shelter a prayer book.

Some say we come heralding
a troop of angels
that the stone seeded well
never truly runs dry.

Do you believe this
that every rag laced with strychnine
we've ever been offered
at one time or another
was meant as a kiss?

Part Four

Flame

You still believe in fairies

that come at night
snatch a baby tooth off the pillow
leave pennies
maybe even a handwritten note

but few people know this
witness the glint in your eye
bigger than money
see past your thin dress
unruly hair.

You still believes in fairies
rocks that wink
a river with voices
sneak out late night
when nobody needs you
tempt the moon into my pocket
reimagine the places I've been
things I've lost
turn what is skeletal, parched
into a meadow of newborns.

We were being coerced

squeezed out of our vanilla bean forest
our folk tales and frog pond
our penny loafers and pleats
being told to eat fast
gobble.

I almost swallowed a fish bone
in my haste.

We were being told to clump things
become the readymade dress
polished brand name.

But my mother had already passed
beyond the field of merchants.

Now every river calls my name
calls my name
moon tinged
sentient.

We propagate stories

no unruly clans
acrimonious sunset

people them with moats and lovers
kingdoms where animals speak
the earth draws poems
from the river.

At first it is difficult
to find our way
turn feldspar into violets
our voice into an open stairway

but now we curl the moon
into a star's cruise ship
train dogs to leap
tired shoes to fly
orchids to rise up deathless

train the man
with the arrows
how to turn target practice
into cake.

She is wearing her palomino shoes

the ones that kiss blind
offer up a dessert plate
don't settle for house arrest
the careful coat
contemptuous nosegays.

They are the night's blue field
beyond the voice's strangle
scout down the moon in a chaste dress.

She is wearing her poor girl's caviar
her palomino shoes
with their no attitude desire
to stomp over bridges
crib the stars
be the *click, click, click*
inside the dark's symphony.

But it wasn't always like this
the blind leading the blind
into a sympathetic room
wasn't always wild iris and daisies
the night with her showy tongue
draping the river
the shoes with the choice fit
willing landscape
the lover who lets you waltz
all over her body
unperturbed
even in a pair of fallen heels.

The holly that has scratched its mark

across my skin
scribed its name
binds me with a love
that is never easy
never just a wreath of birds
clutch of berries.

All night I lay awake
ponder my past
the sky's somnolence
moon's habit of return
the way loss can shelter
a prayer book.

Could it be the holly that has scratched
its mark on my pale skin
is testament to the perilous
is the reason I will reenter your house
dab the blood off my arm
let you come to me
early afternoon
September in the strangle of a heat wave

press your naked body to me
not as a train wreck
but something soft, emptied
a desolate song
half anointed rose petal?

We opened the gates

let the horses loose from their
cultivated field
time honored racetrack
let them take up their will
allow the force of nature
to carry them.
No one thanked us.

At first the horses seemed leery
after all who would lead them
from here to there
groom their mane
offer up oats
an afternoon canter

but over time their bodies loosened
hooves grew unfettered
the far off hills
untried landscape
rustled with a curious claim.

We opened the gates
just as I would want you to do.
Set me loose to my own fables.
The girl who conferences with trees
wears the night as more than a shin guard.

Like me, the horses were bred careful
for speed, endurance
bred to jump over fences
move forceful ahead of the crowd.

I know what it is to jump over fences.
To finally be free.

In the penitentiary of desire

my lips are a floodgate
the night speaks in satin and tailspins
the rump of my body runs along
the rim of your fender
finds the willing landscape
that never needs to crush a nosegay.

In the penitentiary of desire
the weather can turn icy
strip a woman of her clothes
erase the door marked spring
before she even enters.

I memorize your crimped words
desert flowers, shave cream
memorize poems, many poems
tuck orphaned stars in my bed

call to you
call to you
my body
a season of fledgling roses.

Troubles drop on my pillow

I can hear them thump
brides without a home
birds without a season.

And as for the wind
it hounds the fig tree
makes ragged my hair
the yard
the cottonwoods.

Some days I weave a nest
on the far shore
stitch my hands
offer you up grape leaves
honey

some days my dress rides
the dark's soiled seam
words carry salt

troubles drop, drop, drop
into your mouth's well
turn pearl.

We have come single file

a *processional*
this desire to kiss the past
salve the future
give up what no longer serves
be christened with flame.

Some of us are in pale white
almost ethereal
others carry the wind
clipped words
the grief the night sings.

We cup candles
watch them flicker
rise and fall.
After the evocation
there will be plates of cheese
bread, tomato
soothsaying
a maze.

We have come single file
like monks sliding across the sand
in slow motion.
The moon has yet to marry me.
The stars thread the sky with a thin ribbon.
The waves repeat and repeat.

Every story I tell from here on
will hold the shadow of dark water
a penchant for flame
hold the knowledge of having been
once buried in sand
dug out
reclaimed.

She had resurrected a pole star

Cassiopeia, the seventh sister in her lime dress
annexed the night with its half dozed moon
calamine, thorn fields

told her lover – *be still, be still*
as if we are empty cups in wait
for the earth's seedbed.

Things came and went.
The burial ground of the dead
fleeced by robbers.

She memorized the sky
the barn's tilted weight
the lamp's vigilance.

And as for her lover
he was born of the crooked bones
of the yew tree
knew the wind's salt
the sun's appetite to singe
the perils of thwarted summer

opened his mouth beyond
tainted fruit
let the ants, the grubs travel him
and her lips
burned on his lips
clean, joyous
as a sanctified Jesus.

The rain won't let up

is a season of wintering over
cups of splash on the fig's palm leaves.
I am pressed to the window
watch water drip from the holly
clutch what light I can find.

Are some seasons mere prelude
a rehearsal before the real one sets in
or restitution for what's been left behind?
I know the demolition ball that smashes
wood and metal into rubble
know how our lawn refuses to cup seed
grows spotty grass, weed, bald spots
that the angry fist of my father didn't solve things
know a girl's wordless goodbyes can happen
years before the dark claims her

know the sodden machinery that grinds
the chimp trained to be a dazzle of cymbals
the sun's discursive eye over the roses
know animals get maimed in the name of science.

All week rain has been hammering this place
into a grey swamp.
The blackberry bushes we dug up
traced back to their roots
sniped and tugged
carry a will of their own
grow back as if they are deathless.
I know when the rain drums
the layers of river rock we spread out
turn slick, deep toned, an ancient song
that what we promised won't always save
that someday the lowly, simple will inherit the earth
cup a bucket of nothing god turns silver.

This June will not come back
nor my children who have moved on
to find their own place in the world
nor the lovers I once hoped would save me.
And as for the rain – it can be hazardous
a hard exit, stranded boat with no future
can drench our bodies
dissolve hope of its feast table

rinse the dirt off the rows of lettuce
gleam the leaves of the squash vines
make shiny the metal bars of the swing set
then rust them.

This June will not come back
nor the ancestors who once roamed here
bailed hay, cobbled boots, wrote poems, love notes
exchanged vows, built squat houses, a family
compact dreams, a township.

I once thought I could heal
with goldenseal, feverfew, chamomile
hold history in my hand and not maim
fondle a durable future
once thought I could press poems into your hands
bright as a nosegay, moist kiss
talk about the boy left for dead under the ice
the slippery language of trees
the way some things stay presentient
beyond our claim.

So tell me –
inside the inside of the inside
are we all shining suns
meant to flame?

In the mythology of my life

I have always been rolling down hills
in a box with splintered seams
looking for agates
thin skinned to the cold
bundled in layers of sweater, scarf, jacket
that date me.

Outside Newport
the sand holds crushed shells, crab, pebble
a cigarette wrapper
one rubber wade shoe with a boy's name missing.

And I want to believe
in the holy roller school of redemption
where even the broken find a bridge
no one gets displaced
stricken with premature death
because of their age
the color of their skin
a virus.

But for now we keep our distance
travel along the beach
solitary.
I scratch wet sand
pocket two agates
as if treasure can still come
in small parcels.
It is not too late.

After a while

I didn't know how to follow any catechism
turn the other cheek
offer up my willing
didn't understand how words
turn into shiny pollsters
cotton gusseted over a sharp blade.

It can take years for a life
to fall apart
no more lover, marriage, family, house
years to grow back.

Some acts I would wish on no one
some cruelties crush the nosegays in a girl's soul
take a long time to turn crystal.

I had eaten the salt then the sand
come to know that decency hangs
on a thin thread

the true map work of lovers
is more than dangerous
is holy.

How to Make Love

while looking out the hotel window
at a burnished sky -
first appreciate the view
both this body wrapped around you
and the one of the setting sun
that refuses to die
remember you are at the Oregon coast
where all things are possible

don't let the smallest moment
most delicate nipple elude you
make room for surprises
remember every bed, floor, wall surface
is permissible
lounge in your slovenly
let not the prospect of dinner
tangle of hair
unanswered text message
intrude

make this your once and only
never to be repeated
no remnant of a prickly past
unmoored future
remember fondling is good
and unbridled kisses that
suck and search as they go

be generous with your secrets
know they are well-kept
need no applause
and give thanks
stipple with lemon water

spill wide as a fountain
send pools to harbor fish
prosper crops, shafts of iris

blaze a trail
shower for lovers
something beyond strict belief
territory
knowing
the unhinged

keep this safe in your hands
precious.

My mother captured everything

the world had to offer
as if it was her birthright
the ladybug on the leaf, undersized strawberry
rapt orange of tiger lily, blued spruce tree
quivered.

Sometimes when the dark
drove in a fistful of rain
she kept us up late night retelling stories-
the Guernsey pig turned champion swimmer
whippoorwills that sire moths
the cobbler who reshapes the girl's sod shoe
the dog slipped under the ice
orphaned socks adrift in the river.

My mother captured everything
as if a love affair had already seized her
no man could likely live up
to the girth of the earth's singing.
She wore her low cut dresses
spike heels, peach stained lips
summer and winter
up and down church aisles, city streets
swayed her hips back and forth
across the pint sized yard
as if it was a ballroom.

We grew up inside the iridescent of her
promised never to be sick
lose our lives inside the color of money
promised that even the tin rhinestone rings
out of the mouth of machines
the rubber caterpillars, snakes
the doll with the one lazy brown eye
the notes curled inside fortune cookies

the puppet show made of fingers and flashlight
the corn on the cob dimpled with butter
would stay precious.

My mother captured each offering
as if it was a one and only.
It is for her I see in the dark
take nothing for granted
for her I climb the ladders of despair
drink from the moon's carapace
find clothes drying in the sun
the hummingbird's faithful
babies that hatch out of blue eggs

for her I go out first thing
into the garden
marvel at each new bud
leaf, industrious bee
the way the basil, tomato plants, onions
unfurl their stalks and globes
give themselves away to us
free.

My arm is the arm you write on

scribble in blue ink
sometimes purple
as if dissatisfied with your fate
or else unclaimed by it
as if my skin is given up to your cause
my own life no trophy.

I am not always partial to being a tabloid
for the dead's wish list
hearsay, cramped past
need to tap terrestrial onto thin paper.

You worry for the maimed child
forgotten widow
heart failure, cancer
warn of chicanery
slippery words, slush funds
debauchery amid the roses.

My arm is the arm dead folks write on
scribe their regrets, wisdom.
I try to convince you I am
the least of your prospects
the one in the fallen dress
but you do not listen
blue my arm up and down
till I am a meadow of inked snow
unruly daisies.

We are gathering honeysuckle

as if it will turn the crowded day
from canker
debunk the sky of its cloud story
inspire the sullen boy to give up his sling
find a new version of sunrise.

It is July.
Time of my birthday
when the world stops its weary want
when even the grass flirts
rises into a bright crown of candles.

If I once believed the earth only confirms
lays down her breast benevolent for us
now I see fish washed out of the sea
famine and poultices
canary yellow rubbed against a knife blade

like to watch over drowned things
help them travel the world
as more than a mortuary
bake cake
work to keep the dead in nutrition
gather honeysuckle
supper your grave.

The earth is turning light

into the Fatima of roses
the fragrance of lavender
lobelia that cascade purple
thick as a waterfall
petals of orange, sword red, fuchsia.
Even the slender bamboo leaves
so elegant in their clay pot
wave as if they can't resist
the earth throws kisses.

And having crested my heart
with your green tattoos
death, lamentation
I sit still
watch you tap excess
out of the most humble keys.

Even my dog can't resist
sprawls beside me
under the sky's blue dress
takes in the clematis, honeysuckle
as they wind their bodies
up and over the porch rail

what do they say to us
what do they say?

I have seen the eye of God waving

making a frenzied fuss on the subway platform
just when I thought I'd become sturdy, anonymous
able to mind my own business, not stand out

have seen you clutch my weekend suitcase
sling bag of words
squeeze them of rainwater
cause the child in the worn stroller
to turn his head sideways
ponder the avenues of my face.

I have seen you ruffle the leaves
make ragged the wind's polite speech
cause the old man to give up his hat to the pavement

have seen you seep into my tea water
wedge between the buttered toast and the jelly
alive with a language I can barely hear.

I have seen you wage war on the giants
clip them with a blue scissor
unzip the past of its scare rooms

have watched you in the face of my lover
the way his body slows to meet me
offers up scent of meadow, pear tree

have seen you in the guise of the stranger
amid brackish water, conceit
faith scalded with kerosene.

I have seen the eye of God waving
have you
can we ever forget?

Toni Thomas lives in Portland, Oregon. Her poems have been published in Austria, Spain, New Zealand, Canada, England, Scotland, and Australia. In the United States her work has appeared in over fifty literary magazines including *Prairie Schooner, North Dakota Quarterly, Hayden's Ferry Review, the Minnesota Review, Notre Dame Review, Poetry East,* and more. She has twice been nominated for a Pushcart prize, won several awards and also published two children's books.

Her figurative clay sculptures have been shown in gallery exhibits in Portland and Chicago, displayed in literary magazines, and housed in private collections in the U.S. and England.

Her short documentary *One of Us* was shown at the Trans-ideology: Nostalgia festival in Berlin and at the Museum of Contemporary Art in Taipei.

Since Toni loves to create and sits buried in reams of poems, manuscripts, clay figures and images….she likes to imagine all of them out in the world, swaying wild as the lupine.

tonithomaspoetry.com

www.ingramcontent.com/pod-product-compliance
Lightning Source LLC
Chambersburg PA
CBHW021444080526
44588CB00009B/678